My Little Golden Book About
Philadelphia

By Jennifer Dussling
Illustrated by Lenny Wen

A GOLDEN BOOK • NEW YORK

Text copyright © 2022 by Penguin Random House LLC
Cover and interior illustrations copyright © 2022 by Lenny Wen
All rights reserved. Published in the United States by Golden Books, an imprint of
Random House Children's Books, a division of Penguin Random House LLC, 1745 Broadway,
New York, NY 10019. Golden Books, A Golden Book, A Little Golden Book, the G colophon,
and the distinctive gold spine are registered trademarks of Penguin Random House LLC.
rhcbooks.com
Educators and librarians, for a variety of teaching tools, visit us at RHTeachersLibrarians.com
Library of Congress Control Number: 2021930918
ISBN 978-0-593-37470-2 (trade) — ISBN 978-0-593-37471-9 (ebook)
Printed in the United States of America
10 9 8 7 6 5 4 3 2 1

YO, welcome to **Philadelphia**—"Philly" for short, or the City of Brotherly Love. I'm Franklin the Groundhog, and this is my hometown. Want to see what I love about this city? I'll show you! Just give me a minute to get a cheesesteak. . . .

What? Don't tell me you've never had a cheesesteak. You've been missing out! It's one thing Philly is famous for, especially here on **South Street**. Order one with onions and "whiz"— whiz is the cheese in the cheesesteak. Yum!

Did you know Philadelphia is a port city? It sits on the **Delaware River**. Sometimes I just hang out by the water and watch the boats pass by.

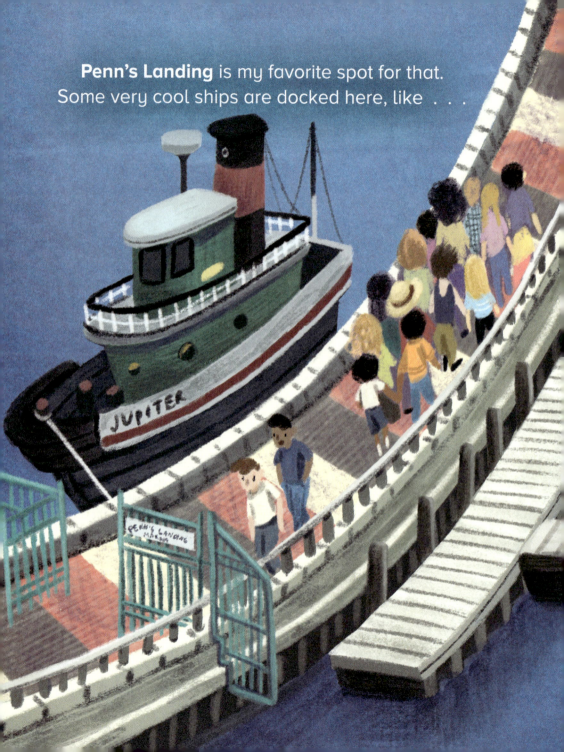
Penn's Landing is my favorite spot for that. Some very cool ships are docked here, like . . .

the U.S.S. *Olympia* from the Spanish-American War, a submarine from World War II, and Philly's oldest tugboat, *Jupiter*.

Let's pop over to **Independence Hall**, the heart and soul of Philadelphia. During the summer of 1776, the founders of our country came together in this brick building to sign the Declaration of Independence. By signing it, they vowed that the American colonies would fight for their freedom from England.

Back then, the **Liberty Bell** hung in the building's steeple. Now it has its own special home. The Liberty Bell is a famous symbol of freedom—and is known for the big crack running up its side.

Want to hear it ring? Sorry, that's not gonna happen. That's how it cracked!

In 1776, General George Washington asked Betsy Ross to sew a flag for our new country—at least, that's the story *I* heard.

No one knows for sure if Betsy Ross actually lived in what's now known as the **Betsy Ross House**, but the building is a must-see stop on any Philly tour. (Only the Liberty Bell is more popular!)

What was it like to live here that long ago? Down the block, houses built between 1703 and 1836 still line a historic cobblestone street called **Elfreth's Alley**. Walking along it is like traveling back in time!

All this history is making me HUNGRY! Good thing we're near **Reading Terminal Market**. It has over one hundred stalls, where we can buy everything from cheese to fruit to fish to flowers. How about some ice cream?

I'll meet you at the giant clothespin afterward.

You found it! This clothespin sculpture, which is forty-five feet tall, was made to celebrate the two-hundredth birthday of our country. Pretty cool, huh?

A lot of the nitty-gritty of running the city happens here in **City Hall**. See the statue of William Penn, the founder of Philadelphia, at the top?

For a long time, nobody in Philly built buildings taller than Mr. Penn's hat. After that tradition was broken, Philly sports teams didn't win a championship for two decades. Finally, in 2007, a small William Penn statue was stuck atop the newest tallest building, and—*bing, bam!*—the next year, the Philadelphia Phillies won the World Series!

I feel a real personal connection with Philly's oldest science museum, the **Franklin Institute**. Nope, it's not named after me! It's named for Benjamin Franklin. You know, the dude with the key and the kite?

While we're here, let's walk through the giant heart . . .

climb aboard an old train . . .

check out
the four-story
pendulum . . .

and stargaze in the planetarium.

I feel myself getting smarter already!

At the end of the street, seventy-two stone steps lead to the world-famous **Philadelphia Art Museum**. The steps are almost as famous as the museum itself. See, in the movie *Rocky,* this boxer guy runs all the way to the top. That's why everyone calls them the Rocky Steps now.

Race you!

Whew! We'll catch our breath inside.
Amazing paintings, sculptures, furniture—
this place has it all! Yeah, this is the good stuff.

Not far away is the **Philadelphia Zoo**, the oldest zoo in the country. It opened way back in 1874.

Raised and covered trails crisscross the zoo. They're not for people—they're for my buddies the animals. They can stroll from one place to another overhead!

If you're a nature lover like me, nothing beats **Fairmont Park**. People from all over come to hang out, hike, bike, and picnic in this great green space. Don't forget to swing by the **Shofuso Japanese House**. It was built as a gift from Japan to the American people.

A river cuts through the middle of Fairmont Park. See the rowers? Rowing is another classic Philly tradition.

Quick! It's getting dark, the perfect time to see **Boathouse Row**, home of the rowing clubs. At night, each boathouse is outlined in lights. Isn't it pretty?

Now you know exactly why I love Philly. Want to do it all again tomorrow? I never get tired of this city!